NS, ACTIVISM, AIRPLANES
CETS, BLACK PANTHERS
ETS, BUILDINGS ...ES
, DOTS, DUNSMUIR HO..SE
FAIRYLAND, FLOWERS
PLAZA, GONDOLAS, GEESE
THEATRE, HENRY J. KAISER
RONS, HIP-HOP, HYPHY
LEVARD, JACK LONDON HOUSE
ANESE ARCH, JUMP ROPE
GARDEN, KINDNESS
LIGHTS, LOVE, MUSEUMS
RMON TEMPLE, NECKLACES
OAK TREES, OBSERVATORY
AC, QUIET, REDWOODS
AIRWAYS, SUNSHINE, SUITS
D, VALENTINES, VICTORIANS
ZEBRAS, ZOO, AND MORE!

ABC OAKLAND

Michael Wertz

Heyday, Berkeley, California

Library of Congress Cataloging-in-Publication Data
Names: Wertz, Michael, author. | Wertz, Michael, illustrator.
Title: ABC Oakland / by Michael Wertz.
Description: Berkeley, California : Heyday, [2017] | Audience: Ages 3 and up.
Identifiers: LCCN 2016018633 | ISBN 9781597143714 (hardcover : alk. paper)
Subjects: LCSH: Oakland (Calif.)—Juvenile literature. | Alphabet
books—Juvenile literature.
Classification: LCC F869.O2 W45 2017 | DDC 979.4/66—dc23
LC record available at https://lccn.loc.gov/2016018633

Book Design: Rebecca LeGates

Orders, inquiries, and correspondence should be addressed to:
Heyday
P.O. Box 9145, Berkeley, CA 94709
(510) 549-3564, Fax (510) 549-1889
www.heydaybooks.com

Printed in Visalia, CA, by Jostens

10 9 8 7 6 5 4 3 2 1

This book is for Mom (who worked at the Kaiser Center for fourteen years), my husband, Andy, our goofy dog, Blue, my art-partners Isabel and Marcos, the Xiques family, and my students and colleagues at CCA (who inspire me every day). This book is for Oakland, the city I love the most.

 is for Aviary,
a home for the birds.

B

is for Broadway,
from College to Third.

is for Cranes standing tall in the sky.

is for Dogs, wagging tails, saying "hi!"

E is for Earthquakes that shake up our town.

F is for Fairyland,
where magic is found.

G

is for Grand, branching off from the lake.

H is for Henry J.,
shaped like a cake.

 is for International.
If you're hungry,
come eat!

J is for Jack London, the square near the fleet.

 **is for Kindness, a wave and a smile.**

L is for Lake Merritt. Come hang out for a while!

 is for Museums,
with so much to see.

N is for Neighbors:
all of us, you and me.

 **is for Ohlone, first people of this land.**

P is for Port, greeting boats big and grand.

is for Quiet
when the fog rolls in.

R is for Redwoods
that sway in the wind.

S is for Stairways
up and down hills.

T is for Tribune Tower.
The view is a thrill!

U

is for Underground:
BART, music, and art.

is for Victorians painted with hearts.

W is for Wheels: all the folks on the move.

 **marks the spot
to get in the groove.**

is for You. What do you love in your town?

OAKLAND ZOO

Z is for Zoo, where Zebras abound!

There's so much to love in our Oakland—it's true.

There's no better city
for you to do you!

MICHAEL WERTZ

is a noted illustrator, professor at the California College of the Arts, and friend to all four-pawed creatures. He hails from the gently rolling hills of Northern Californialand and has been lucky enough to call Oakland his home since 2000. His work has been recognized by *Communication Arts* and *American Illustration,* and he has worked with museums like Oakland Museum of California and the de Young, publications like *The New York Times,* and bands like Camper Van Beethoven. This is his seventh book for kids. To see more of Michael's work, please visit wertzateria.com.

OAKLANDISH

OAKLANDISH started in 2000 as a public art project designed to illuminate Oakland's local history and unique cultural legacy. After years of covert multimedia stunts around the Town, the Oaklandish brand of apparel was introduced to help support our ongoing calendar of public events and annual Oaklandish Innovators Grant program.

Our mission is to spread "local love" by way of our civic pride-evoking tees and accessories, while creating quality inner-city jobs for locals, and giving back to the people and places that maintain our city's trailblazer spirit. In line with this mission, we donate a portion of all proceeds to grassroots nonprofits committed to bettering the Oakland community.

Oaklandish is proud to sponsor this book with Heyday, and together with Heyday will be donating a copy to every kindergarten class in the city of Oakland.

Oaklandish.com

 @oaklandishhq   @0aklandish   /oaklandish

Locations:
Downtown Oakland 1444 Broadway, Oakland, CA
Dimond District 3419 Fruitvale, Oakland, CA

OAKLAND IS HOME TO ACC
APPLES, AVIARY, A'S, AV
BROADWAY, BROWN BE
CRANES, CHINATOWN, DO
EARTHQUAKES, EGRET
FOX THEATER, FRANK OGAV
GRAND AVENUE, GRAND LA
CONVENTION CENTER, I
ICE CREAM, INTERNATIONAL B
JACK LONDON SQUARE, J
KAISER CENTER ROO
LAKE MERRITT, LIBRARY
MOUNTAINVIEW CEMETERY,
NEIGHBORS, NEWTS, NOODL
OHLONE, PORT, POTOI
SALSA DANCING, SECRET S
TRIBUNE TOWER, UNDERGRO
WHEELS, XYLOPHONES, YO